MY FIRST LOOK AT HOLIDAYS

A cat dressed in Christmas ribbons

Christmas

AARON FRISCH

CREATIVE EDUCATION

Jesus's Birthday

A long time ago, a man named Jesus was born. Christians believe Jesus was God's son. They call him "Christ." Christmas is Jesus's birthday. It is on December 25.

Jesus was born in a little barn called a stable. Angels visited him. So did **shepherds** and sheep. He was also visited by three kings who rode camels. At Christmas, some

Christmas

AARON FRISCH

CREATIVE EDUCATION

Published by Creative Education

123 South Broad Street, Mankato, Minnesota 56001

Creative Education is an imprint of The Creative Company

Designed by Rita Marshall

Photographs by Archive Photos, Curtis Martin, Louisa Preston, Mrs. Kevin Scheibel, The

Viesti Collection (Bavaria, Richard Cummins)

Cover illustration © 1996 Roberto Innocenti

Copyright © 2006 Creative Education

Printed in the United States of America

Library of Congress Cataloging-in-Publication Data

Frisch, Aaron. Christmas / by Aaron Frisch.

p. cm. — (My first look at holidays)

ISBN 1-58341-366-9

1. Christmas—Juvenile literature. I. Title.

GT4985.5.F75 2005   394.2663—dc22   2004057096

First edition 9 8 7 6 5 4 3 2 1

CHRISTMAS

Jesus's Birthday

A long time ago, a man named Jesus was born. Christians believe Jesus was God's son. They call him "Christ." Christmas is Jesus's birthday. It is on December 25.

Jesus was born in a little barn called a stable. Angels visited him. So did **shepherds** and sheep. He was also visited by three kings who rode camels. At Christmas, some

A church window showing a Christmas scene

people set up statues of Jesus and his visitors. These are called Nativity scenes.

Most Christians go to church on Christmas. They listen to Bible stories about Jesus's birth. Churches may be decorated with **evergreen** branches and red flowers. Green and red are the colors of Christmas.

Some people ring

bells at Christmas.

The song "Jingle Bells"

is about Christmas bells.

TREES LIT WITH STRINGS OF CHRISTMAS LIGHTS

Trees and Lights

Many people get ready for Christmas early in December. They put up decorations. The most famous one is the Christmas tree. This is an evergreen tree that people set up in their homes. They hang colored lights and **ornaments** on it. They may put a star or angel decoration on top.

There are more than

300 different Christmas songs.

Many people like

"Silent Night" the best.

PEOPLE ONCE USED CANDLES TO LIGHT THEIR TREES

People put Christmas lights on trees outside, too. Or they may hang them on houses. Some people put candles in windows. In cold parts of the world, it snows around Christmas. This is why people talk about having a "White Christmas."

CHRISTMAS FUN

Christmas is a happy time. People wish others a "Merry Christmas." Some people send Christmas cards to their friends. People sing and listen to songs called Christmas carols.

A HOUSE DECORATED FOR CHRISTMAS

Some people eat special foods at Christmas. Many families eat turkey and potatoes. Eggnog is a special Christmas drink. Many kids like eating candy canes.

Presents are a big part of Christmas. People make or buy presents for their friends and families. They wrap them in colorful paper and put them under the Christmas tree. It is fun trying to guess what is inside!

Some people make

special gingerbread cookies

at Christmas. They

make houses smell good!

Santa Claus

Who makes Christmas extra special? Santa Claus! A long time ago, a **holy** man named Saint Nicholas gave kids presents. Later, people called him "Santa Claus."

Santa Claus is a fat man with a white beard. Kids believe that he brings presents on Christmas Eve (the night before Christmas). He climbs down the chimney and puts toys

AN OLD DRAWING SHOWING SAINT NICHOLAS

under the tree. Then he flies away in a big sled pulled by reindeer.

Seven days after Christmas is another **holiday**. It is January 1: New Year's Day. Because of this, many people say "Merry Christmas and a Happy New Year!"

Kids in Britain call
Santa Claus "Father Christmas."
Kids in France call him
"Pere Noel."

SANTA CLAUS BRINGS PRESENTS TO GOOD KIDS

Hands-on: Christmas Chains

A Christmas chain is a fun way to count the days until Christmas!

What You Need

Red and green paper
Scissors
Tape

What You Do

1. Ask a grown-up to help you cut the paper into strips about the size of a candy bar. Make as many strips as there are days until Christmas.
2. Loop one strip of paper into a circle and tape it. This is the first link. Loop another strip through the first one and tape it. Do this with all of the strips to make a chain.
3. Tear one link off each day until Christmas!

DECORATING FOR CHRISTMAS CAN BE LOTS OF FUN

INDEX

WORDS TO KNOW

evergreen—plants that have pointy leaves and stay green all year

holiday—a special day that happens every year

holy—having to do with God

ornaments—small, colorful things used to decorate Christmas trees

shepherds—people who watch over sheep and keep them safe

READ MORE

Moore, Clement C., and Mary Engelbreit. *The Night Before Christmas*. New York: HarperCollins, 2003.

Pingry, Patricia, and Lorraine Wells. *The Story of Christmas*. New York: Candy Cane Press, 2001.

Sadler, Judy Ann, and June Bradford. *Christmas Crafts from Around the World*. Toronto: Kids Can Press, 2003.

EXPLORE THE WEB

Christmas Crafts for Kids http://www.enchantedlearning.com/crafts/christmas

Christmas for Kids http://www.rexanne.com/xmas-kids.html

Merry-Christmas.com http://www.merry-christmas.com/kids_zone.htm